Don't Fear the End
YOUR HOPE OF HEAVEN IS SECURE

Pastor David Scharf

Published by Straight Talk Books
P.O. Box 301, Milwaukee, WI 53201
800.661.3311 · timeofgrace.org

Copyright © 2016 Time of Grace Ministry

All rights reserved. This publication may not be copied, photocopied, reproduced, translated, or converted to any electronic or machine-readable form in whole or in part, except for brief quotations, without prior written approval from Time of Grace Ministry.

Unless otherwise indicated, Scripture is taken from THE HOLY BIBLE, NEW INTERNATIONAL VERSION®, NIV®. Copyright © 1973, 1978, 1984, 2011 by Biblica, Inc. ® Used by permission. All rights reserved worldwide.

Printed in the United States of America
ISBN: 978-1-942107-45-3

TIME OF GRACE *is a registered mark of Time of Grace Ministry.*

Contents

Introduction 4

What Will Heaven Be Like? 5

How Do I Get There? 10

Will God Really Forgive Me? 24

What Am I Here For? 30

What Happens When I Die? 38

When Is the Last Day Going to Happen? 43

Introduction

Do you know what *Thanatophobia* is? Whether you're familiar with that word or not, I'll bet that you suffer at least a little from it. We all do to some degree. Thanatophobia is the fear of death. Death is something that will befall every person who walks the face of this earth, unless of course, Jesus comes first. And there's another common fear: judgment day! Most think of judgment day as the day when all of their most hidden sins will be revealed. What do most people feel when faced with the thought of judgment day? Fear, anxiety, guilt . . . none of which are pleasant!

So, do we have to fear death and judgment day? In this book, we find the answers on the basis of God's Word. We see that Jesus comforts us with the words, "Do not be afraid," when it comes to this question. And the reason we don't need to be afraid might surprise you. Our assurance doesn't come from our great lives or our great faith. Our assurance comes from Jesus, who has secured our salvation from beginning to end. Come along on this journey as we consider topics like heaven, faith, God's means of working that faith, and questions about judgment day.

David J. Scharf

What Will Heaven Be Like?

When I was about five or six years old, I remember asking my mother, "Mom, what will heaven be like?" I love my mother, but the answer she gave could not have been worse. She said, "Well, Davey Boy (she still calls me that, by the way), heaven will be like church ALL THE TIME." I heard that and thought, *"Oh, you have to be kidding me! Heaven's going to be so boring!"* I remember praying after that, *"Jesus, you know I'm going to Great America on Saturday—do you think you could hold off on my dying until Sunday or Monday?"* My mother meant well. But now that I'm older and more versed in Scripture, I realize her description was not actually that bad.

In the book of Revelation, God gives us a picture of what heaven will be like. It describes the believers in heaven from every nation, tribe, people, and language, standing before the throne of Jesus, holding palm branches in their hands, and shouting out their worship: **"Salvation belongs to our God, who sits on the throne, and to the Lamb"** (Revelation 7:10). God goes on to describe the perfect bliss of heaven for his believers: **"Therefore, they are before the**

> God gives us a picture of what heaven will be like.

throne of God and serve him day and night in his temple; and he who sits on the throne will shelter them with his presence. 'Never again will they hunger; never again will they thirst. The sun will not beat down on them,' nor any scorching heat. For the Lamb (i.e., Jesus) **at the center of the throne will be their shepherd; 'he will lead them to springs of living water.' 'And God will wipe away every tear from their eyes'"** (Revelation 7:15-17).

Isn't that beautiful? The word that the Bible uses for "serve" in these verses is the word for "worship." So yes, Mom, it will be like church all the time . . . but the sermon will never be boring, the musicians will all be stellar, and there won't be any people glaring at you because your kid is making too much noise. But that word for "serve" is not limited to worship. So what else will heaven be like?

The great Reformation theologian Martin Luther once wrote a letter to his elementary school-aged son. In it he described heaven like this: "I know of a pretty, beautiful, and cheerful garden where there are many children wearing little golden coats. They pick up fine apples, pears, cherries, and yellow and blue plums under the trees; they sing, jump, and are merry. They also have nice ponies with golden reins and silver saddles . . . and when they are all together, they will also get whistles, drums, lutes, and all kinds of other stringed instruments; and they will also dance, and shoot with little crossbows" (Theodore Hartwig, *The Past Speaks for Itself*, page 119). What was Luther's point? He wasn't trying to give specifics as biblical truth. He was trying to explain to his young son that heaven will be perfectly happy by using descriptions of things that bring little boys happiness.

As a parish pastor, when a member of my congregation passed away, I would sometimes entertain the pious speculation that happens at times like those. If the Christian was a big hunter, I might say, "Right now Bob is enjoying the biggest Cabella's ever built!" Or if the person loved game shows, I might say, "Ruth just found out what it feels like to win the showcase showdown on heaven's *Price Is Right*." The family gets the point—their loved one is perfectly happy in heaven.

> Their loved one is perfectly happy in heaven.

One of the best-known sections of Scripture that's often read at funerals or committals describes heaven this way: **"I heard a loud voice from the throne saying, 'Look! God's dwelling place is now among the people, and he will dwell**

with them. They will be his people, and God himself will be with them and be their God. He will wipe every tear from their eyes. There will be no more death or mourning or crying or pain, for the old order of things has passed away'" (Revelation 21:3,4). I think that's interesting. When the Bible describes heaven, it so often describes what is *not* going to be there. There will be no more tears of sadness that so often stream down our faces. There will be no more death, which comes for each one of us here on this earth. You won't hear the dirge of mourners or the wailing of despair. There won't be any cancer, no broken bones, no financial ruin, no hurts or aches, no feelings of disappointment or failure . . . no pain.

The Bible most often describes what is *not* going to be there. Why do you suppose that is? I think it's because it's what we can relate to. If the Bible were to describe the perfections of heaven, it would be like a rocket scientist trying to tell me about the intricacies of his work in Swahili—it's not in my experience base; I don't even know that language! The same goes for the perfection of heaven—I've never experienced perfection before. So what does Jesus do to comfort us? He tells us all the things that so trouble us and assures us: "They won't be there. Every tear, gone."

The Bible tells about all these things that won't

be there and one thing that will: Jesus. And that's enough. And because Jesus will be there, we will be perfectly happy. The best answer I think I've ever heard to the question, What will we do in heaven? is this: "I don't know exactly what we will be doing in heaven; all I know is that whatever we are doing, we *will not* wish that we were doing anything else."

In one word, what will heaven be like? *Awesome.* And I don't mean that in the teenybopper way that that word is used to describe anything from a majestic Grand Canyon view to the fact that someone gave them ketchup with their French fries. I mean AWEsome. I think we'll spend the first one thousand years of our time in heaven standing there gap-jawed trying to take it all in. That's what the Bible says heaven is like.

How Do I Get There?

Life is full of big questions, but maybe *What will heaven be like?* is not the question that eats at you. I'll bet it's related though. Does it go something like this: Will I be there? Do I need to be afraid? How do I get there? As with so many big questions in life, the Bible has the answers to those too.

Jesus says in Matthew chapter 5: **"Be perfect, therefore, as your heavenly Father is perfect"** (verse 48). Just be as perfect as God, and you will have no worries. Do you feel better now? No! Neither do I! Be perfect? Do you know how many wrong things you and I can do before we would be termed "imperfect"? Well, it's the same answer as this question: How many pinpricks can a balloon take before it's popped? One. Just one. Not even Mary Poppins would make the cut (i.e., practically perfect in every way).

Jesus went on to explain what it means to be perfect. When asked to explain which is the most important commandment, Jesus replied, **"Love the Lord your God with all your heart and with all your soul and with all your mind. . . . Love your neighbor as yourself"** (Matthew 22:37,39). Do you see what Jesus was doing? He was summing up the entire Ten Commandments into one word: *Love*. In other words, all of the commandments in the law of God are important.

This might sound strange to say at first, but bear with me. The Bible describes two ways to get to heaven. Either you get there by your perfect life (i.e., the law) or you get there by Jesus' perfect life (i.e., the gospel). However, for every person who has ever walked the face of this earth with the exception of Jesus, there remains only one way: through Jesus' perfect life.

So what is the point of the law? The Bible says, **"We know that whatever the law says, it says to those who are under the law, *so that every mouth may be silenced* and the whole world held accountable to God. Therefore no one will be declared righteous in God's sight by the works of the law; rather, *through the law we become conscious of sin*"** (Romans 3:19,20). The law's main purpose is to show us we can't keep it.

Imagine that you came to my church and I stood up and said, "Hi, everyone! I'm Tom Cruise, and I'll be preaching the sermon today." Obviously, I'm not Tom Cruise. You know it, the rest of the people in church know it, and the whole world knows it. But at that moment, I don't. How are you going to convince me that I'm not Tom Cruise? Be nice! I'm sure you'd start by saying that I'm taller than Tom Cruise is. You could tell me that I didn't star in movies or that I don't look like him or that I'm not a Scientologist. And I could dodge every one of your attempts. I could simply say, "I look shorter in the movies. I did star in all those movies. I do look like him. I converted to Christianity." You can try to convince me all you want until you are blue in the face, and it wouldn't work. Do you know how you could convince me? Show me a mirror. Suddenly, when I look at myself in a mirror, I can have no excuse. That's what God's law does. It forces me to look at myself in the mirror of God's law and see all the wrinkles and gashes and imperfections about myself.

And that function of the law is a good thing! Because sometimes we don't even realize that what we are doing is wrong unless we see it clearly in God's Word. Paul goes on to say, **"I would not have known what sin was had it not been for the law. For I would not have known what coveting really was if the law had not said, 'You shall not covet'"** (Romans 7:7). The law in the Bible is a good thing because it shows us what sin is.

> Sometimes we don't even realize that what we are doing is wrong unless we see it clearly in God's Word.

Recently, I was guest preaching at a church about two hours from my house on a Saturday night. The most direct route to get there was to pass through multiple little towns on two-lane roads. If you've ever travelled on roads like that you know that the speed limits change from 55 mph to 45 to 35 as you enter into town and from 35 to 45 to 55 mph as you leave town.

By the time I got back on the road to get home, it was dark. I was tooling along thinking that I was going the speed limit of 45 mph, when I saw a car spin around and ride up close to my bumper. After a heart-pounding couple of seconds, the police car's lights turned on and the officer pulled me over. He asked me, "Do you know why I pulled you over?" I said that I must have been going too fast but that I thought I was going 45 mph. He said, "But the problem is that you are in a 35 mph zone." I missed the posted law saying it was 35 mph. Then he finally asked me the question I had been waiting for: "Where are you coming from?" I got to answer, "Well, I just preached at a church in a town down the road and was heading back home." And then his eyes glanced back to the hanger in back with my robe on it. No ticket was given. "Thank you, police officer . . . thank you, Lord!" My point in sharing that is not so you put a preacher's robe in the back of your car. My point is that without the law, I would have never known I was doing something wrong! The point of the law is to show us our sin.

And we don't even come close to keeping all of God's law. The Bible says, **"There is no difference . . . for all have sinned and fall short of the glory of God"** (Romans 3:22,23). Let's say that you, your friend, and I decide to go to the Grand Canyon. The Grand Canyon is up to 18 miles wide and about 1 mile deep. And while we are there looking out over it, I say, "I know! I've got a great idea! Let's jump over the canyon!" And you say, "Great idea, Dave. . . . You go first." So I get a running start and begin my jump, but on my jump, I trip over a rock and make it about a foot over the cliff. What happens to me? I go bouncing down the side of the canyon! Next your friend takes a running start and gets a great jump of 20 feet. What happens to your friend? Same as me! Then it's your turn, and you have some sort of tailwind because you set a world record of 50 feet. What happens to you? Same as me! So how close did we come to jumping over the 18 mile-wide canyon? Not even close!

The same is true when it comes to the glory or the praise of God. **"All have sinned and fall short of the glory** (i.e., praise) **of God"** (Romans 3:23). We like to compare ourselves with others when it comes to God's law, but there's no point. My jump of 1 foot was like an axe murderer's attempt at life. He doesn't make it far in his attempt at receiving the glory of God. Your friend's jump of 20 feet might be like a "normal" person's attempt. It's further than the axe murderer, but it's still not even close. Your jump of 50 feet could compare to Mother Teresa's attempt at earning God's praise—it went further, but it's still *so* far short. And that's God's point. Comparisons to other people do us no good. God wants us to compare our lives to the perfection he requires. The Bible says, **"Whoever keeps the whole law and yet stumbles at just one point is guilty of breaking all of it"** (James 2:10). It doesn't matter if we've stepped off the cliff a lot or a little; the result is still the same.

Okay, these have been a rough couple of pages. There's not a lot of good news there! Why did we have to go through those pages? Because we need to let the law of God work on our hearts to show us something. The law shows us we have a need. The only response we can give to the law is to object, "But, Jesus, I can't be what you want me to be. If that's what you want from me, then forget it! Nobody's perfect!" Nobody? The great church father Augustine once prayed, "God, give me whatever you demand of me, then demand anything you want." In other words, if you want me to be perfect, then you're going to have to give it to me. The Bible does say, **"The wages of sin is death,"** but don't forget how that passage goes on: **"But the gift of God is eternal life in Christ Jesus, our Lord"** (Romans 6:23).

If God must be the one to give it to me, how *does* God give me heaven? Listen to what he tells us in the Bible: **"He** [Jesus] **is the atoning sacrifice for our sins, and not only for ours but also for the sins of the whole world"** (1 John 2:2). The whole world! Isn't that comforting? It's even more comforting than if God had used your name in that passage. Let's say your name is John Smith and you read in the Bible, "Jesus died for the sins of John Smith." Would you be comforted? Not necessarily. You'd always wonder which of the thousands of John Smiths who have lived God was talking about. But since the Bible says, "Jesus died for the sins of the world," you know he means you because you are part of the whole world that Jesus died for.

So how does that gift of Jesus' perfect life and death become mine? God says, **"For God so loved the world . . ."** Just pause there for a moment. The world is full of evil and wickedness and hatred—and God loved that? Yes. And you and I are part of the world that God loved. He loved us before we were even born. **"God so loved the world that he gave his one and only Son . . ."** Please, let's never gloss over that astonishing phrase. It expresses a truth of God's heart. I have one son. I love him. I would not give him over to death for you or anyone else. Even if I had ten sons, I wouldn't give one of them up! But God did. The truth of God's heart is that he loved you so much that he gave his Son . . . so that he could have you. Jesus lived the perfect life you couldn't, and then he loved you to death on a cross. He earned the gift, and now the passage goes on to tell us how God gives it to us: **"God so loved the world that he gave his one and only Son, that *whoever believes in him* shall not perish but have eternal life"** (John 3:16).

God gives you the blessings of what Jesus did for you, including heaven, through faith. What's faith? Faith is believing. Faith is something that receives God's blessings. Picture a water tower that supplies water to a town. Imagine that you live in that town. The tower has enough water to supply all you need. So you go to Home Depot, you get a new sink, you plop it in the middle of your living room, and you turn on the faucet. What happens? Nothing comes out. Why? I thought there was enough water for you? Yes, but you need the pipes to be hooked up to it. Faith

> God gives you the blessings of what Jesus did for you, including heaven, through faith.

is like those pipes. Jesus died for the sins of the whole world. Through faith, that becomes yours so that you can say, "Jesus died for my sins."

Uh-oh, it sounds like we're back into needing to do something to get to heaven. Is faith something we have to "do"? No! God says, **"As for you, you were dead in your transgressions and sins"** (Ephesians 2:1). He describes us as dead. When I taught elementary school religion class, I used to find a dead cricket and put it in a container. I would then introduce the class to my friend Fred the cricket. I'd shake the container, and a couple of Fred's legs would fall off. I'd say, "What is Fred's problem?" "Fred is dead," they would all say. Then I'd go up to someone in the front row and say, "Now, if I lift this cover, are you afraid Fred will jump out at you." And they'd say, "No." "Why not?" "Because he's dead!" It's an obvious point. Dead people cannot do anything . . . they're dead. Dead people cannot come to life on their own. They cannot choose to believe or have faith . . . they're dead. If you came to my funeral visitation and you saw me lying up there in the casket, you wouldn't take a $50 bill and wave it in my face and say, "It's all yours, Dave. All you have to do is grab it!" No, that would be crazy . . . and a little mean! What would it take for Fred to jump out of the container? What would it take for me to grab that $50 bill? A miracle. And that's precisely what God gives to you and me.

The apostle Paul says in Ephesians 2:8,9, **"It is by grace you have been saved, through faith—and this is not from yourselves, it is the gift of God—not by works, so that no one can boast."** Faith is described as a gift that God gives to you and me. The gift is our gift, but we don't get to take credit for it. It is similar to if a friend were to give you an incredible present and you were to open it up and say, "I love it! I'm so glad I got it for myself." If you were to take credit for the gift, the friend might just take it back! In the same way, we can't take credit for the gift of faith. It's our faith (i.e., we believe), but the reason is that it was given to us by God.

> *Faith is described as a gift that God gives to you and me.*

How does God give the gift of faith? Romans 10:17 says, **"Consequently, faith comes from hearing the message, and the message is heard through the word about Christ."** When you hear about Jesus and what he's done for you, God, the Holy Spirit, works that trust in your heart: **"No one can say, 'Jesus is Lord,' except by the Holy Spirit"** (1 Corinthians 12:3). So I'll ask you, do you believe that Jesus died on the cross to take away the sins of the world, including yours? If the answer is yes, then you know the Holy Spirit has worked faith in your heart. It's not something you had to do or choose. It is God's gift to you! Isn't that freeing? Someone once said, "The hardest thing for a believer to believe is that he really believes." That's so true when we look at ourselves. If we look at how much we think we believe, we will always have to wonder if we really believe. But when we doubt our faith, we instead look at Jesus' cross and say, "Did he die for me?" The answer is yes! My assurance and my confidence don't come from inside of me but from the objective truth of what Jesus has done for me.

The news about Jesus, who he is and what he's done, is what the Bible calls the gospel, which means "Good News." You can see why the apostle Paul says so forcefully, **"I am not ashamed of the gospel, because it is the power of God that brings salvation to everyone who believes"** (Romans 1:16). How does God give us heaven? It is by the Holy Spirit using that powerful gospel message to work faith in our hearts. That is the miracle that we need! You can see why the Bible says, **"When you were dead in your sins . . . God made you alive with Christ"** (Colossians 2:13). You are a walking miracle!

After all, why did God give us the Bible? There are some who say that we have God's Word so that we can get rich. Preachers will tell you that God wants you to have whatever you want and that if you pray hard enough and live right, he'll give it to you. But that's not the purpose of the Bible—not rich in a worldly sense. James says, **"Has not God chosen those who are poor in the eyes of the world to be rich in faith and to inherit the kingdom he promised those who love him?"** (James 2:5).

There are some who say that we have God's Word because God wants us to be happy. In my experience, the only people who say, "God just wants me to be happy" are the ones who want to make themselves feel better about living in a way contrary to what God says. Instead, Jesus says, **"Whoever wants to be my disciple must deny themselves and take up** (not his retirement fund, not his house up north, but . . .) **their cross daily and follow me"** (Luke 9:23). Jesus says the Christian life is going to be hard! He tells us to deny ourselves. Think of all the words that start with *self*. *Self-image, self-esteem, self-worth, self-confidence,* etc. Jesus says deny self—that's hard! He says to take up a cross—that's not a happy thing! The purpose of the Bible is not to make me happy (joyful, but not necessarily happy).

There are some who think we have God's Word to make us good, moral people. It's interesting to note when parents who have stopped going to church come back to church again. Can you guess when? It's when their children get to Sunday school age and they want them to learn good morals. But again, we've already discussed how "good" we are by ourselves in the eyes of God. You might say that "moral living" is a secondary blessing of following the Bible, but it's not the main purpose.

So what is the purpose of the Bible? The Bible tells us. Toward the end of his beautiful gospel about Jesus' life, death, and resurrection, the apostle John says, **"These are written that you may believe that Jesus is the Messiah, the Son of God, and that by believing you may have life in his name"** (John 20:31). That's it! God gives you his Word to work faith in your heart . . . so that you will be in heaven with him.

Knowing that, what will we now do? We will want to do what God wants us to do not because we have to but because we want to in order to say thank you to God for his gifts. That concept separates Christianity from every other world religion throughout the history of the world. In *every other* religion, we need to do something in order to please God—we have to. In Christianity, we want to do something for God because he already is pleased with us. Our lives are thank-you notes to God. A person doesn't write a thank-you note in order to pay someone back. If I give you a million dollars and I ask you to take out my garbage when I'm out of town, you wouldn't think you were paying me back. You would do it to say thank you.

The Bible says, **"Christ's love compels us, because we are convinced that one died for all, and therefore all died. And he died for all, that those who live should no longer live for themselves but for him who died for them and was raised again"** (2 Corinthians 5:14,15). Can you see the *why*? We're compelled, but not in a forced way. We're compelled in the sense that it's the only thing we feel like doing. What are we compelled by? Christ's love. I will respond in proportion to the love and sacrifice someone shows to me. If you buy me a cup of coffee, I will shake your hand. If you pay off the mortgage on my house, I will kiss your feet! But if you suffer hell for me? Wow! There is nothing I wouldn't do for you. Jesus suffered hell for us on the cross. That's Christ's love. Isn't it compelling? I want to live for him not because I have to but because I've never experienced any love greater than that!

Will God Really Forgive Me?

If you're like me, we need to admit that our lives of thanks so often fall short of what God wants. That leaves us thinking, *"Will God really forgive me?"* True confession time. I struggle with guilt. As much as I try to serve Jesus with my life, I get the thought in my head that God must not be pleased with me. I'm sure you can relate.

When Jesus says that he died for the sins of all, he means you!

God has blessed me with a wife, six kids, and a wonderful job. However, when I'm at work, I feel guilty that I'm not spending enough time with my wife and kids. When I'm with my wife or kids, I keep thinking I should be doing more to be faithful at work. Then add to that the tortured conscience from past failures, and the result is crushing guilt. Whoever said that the mistakes you make when you're 20 will keep you up nights when you're 50 hit the nail on the head (and I'm not even 50 yet!). Will God really forgive me? Will he forgive you?

The answer from the Bible is a resounding, "Yes!" We've already discussed how God gives you his love and forgiveness and mercy through his powerful Word. When Jesus says that he died for the sins of all, he means you! Through his Word, God looks at you and says, "I'm going to take every sin of yours and place it on my Son. He will suffer the hell you deserve in your place. And for you? I'll forgive you and wash you so clean that I'll never remember that you were a sinner." Through his Word, God assures you, "Yes, you are really forgiven! I love you."

But here's the beautiful thing. He doesn't show you his love and forgiveness in just one way. Through Baptism, he assures you that you are forgiven and loved as his child. Acts 2:38 says, **"Repent and be baptized, every one of you, in the name of Jesus Christ for the forgiveness of your sins."** The word "for" expresses the purpose of Baptism. It is so that you receive the *forgiveness* you need so much. The word the Bible uses for forgiveness here is a beautiful word. Literally it means "to send away," and it calls to mind the Day of Atonement in the Old Testament.

The Day of Atonement is the festival you know on your calendar as Yom Kippur. There are many rich pictures of God's love here, but I want to focus on one especially: the scapegoat. On the Day of Atonement, the priest was to take a goat and place his hand over the goat's head and symbolically transfer all the sins of the people onto the goat. Then a man appointed to the task would lead the goat into the desert, and the goat would never be seen again.

Do you see the picture of God's forgiveness? God "sends away" the people's sin. He'll never see that sin again because it is gone. Listen to the beautiful way the psalmist expresses it: **"As far as the east is from the west, so far has he removed our transgressions from us"** (Psalm 103:12) How far is the east from the west? Well, just start walking east. If you are walking east, how far do you have to go before you'll be walking west? Will it ever happen? Never! East and west are infinitely apart—that's how far God has sent away your sin.

I began this section by talking about the guilt we carry around. Watch how God takes away the need for that feeling of guilt through Baptism. **"Baptism that now saves you also—not the removal of dirt from the body but the pledge of a clear conscience toward God. It saves you by the resurrection of Jesus Christ"** (1 Peter 3:21). Baptism gives you the pledge or guarantee of a good conscience toward God. And notice why. Not because you have defeated every demon that plagues you to sin, but because Jesus has, and your baptism connects you to his victorious resurrection.

But perhaps my favorite picture of what Baptism does for us is from Ephesians chapter 5, where the apostle Paul uses the picture of marriage: **"Husbands, love your wives, just as Christ loved the church and gave himself up for her to make her holy, cleansing her by the washing with water through the word, and to present her to himself as a radiant church, without stain or wrinkle or any other blemish, but holy and blameless"** (Ephesians 5:25-27).

Think about a wedding day. Does the bride spend a couple of extra minutes than normal to get ready for that day? Absolutely! Many brides will spend months looking for the perfect dress and jewelry and hours doing their hair and makeup. Now, suppose the bridegroom follows the tradition and doesn't see the bride before the wedding. Picture him standing up front nervously waiting for those doors to open and see his bride. The doors open and she walks into the doorway. What is his first thought? That's easy! *"Wow!"* She takes his breath away because she looks so beautiful. Notice what God says here. Through Baptism, he has made you radiant, without stain or wrinkle or any other blemish. You are holy and blameless in his eyes because he sees the perfection of Jesus. Do you know what he

Through Baptism, God assures you, "Yes, you are really forgiven! I love you."

thinks when he looks at you? *"Wow!"* You take his breath away. Through Baptism, God assures you, "Yes, you are really forgiven! I love you."

And God's not done assuring you of his love and forgiveness! In the Lord's Supper, he gives you himself. Jesus said, **"This is my body. . . . This is my blood of the covenant, which is poured out for many for the forgiveness of sins"** (Matthew 26:26-28). There's that "for" word again, which expresses purpose. The purpose of the Lord's Supper is to assure you that you really are forgiven. Having nothing of this world to give, he gave us himself on the night before he died. What greater assurance can there be that you are forgiven! When you are at the Lord's Table receiving his body and blood, at that moment it is just you and Jesus. Through the Lord's Supper, God assures you, "Yes, you are really forgiven! I love you!"

So God gives you the same love and forgiveness in three ways—through the Word, in your baptism, in his Supper. Is he being redundant since he gives us the same thing in all those ways? Well, wives, is it redundant for your husbands to tell you that they love you over and over? Because when you got married, he promised to love you until you die. That's a promise. So that should be good, right? He should never have to say it again, right? No! Your husband knows that you love to hear it, and he loves to hear it back again and again. And you appreciate that he doesn't just say it but shows it in a variety of ways.

Is Jesus being redundant? Not at all—instead *Jesus knows my heart*. He knows how easily I can doubt his love. Think about it. Perhaps you've sat in church and you've heard the pastor announce, "Your sins are forgiven in the name of the Father and of the Son and of the Holy Spirit." Does Jesus mean you? Absolutely! But you might be thinking to yourself, *"He can't mean me. If he knew what I've done, he wouldn't be saying that. He means the rest who are here."* And so Jesus takes you back to the baptismal font and says, "Remember what I did for you here. I made you—no one else but you at that moment—my child. See, I love you. I forgive you." Does Jesus mean it? Absolutely! But you might think, *"Yeah, but that was a long time ago—I've walked away from you, Jesus. You can't still mean it."* So then, what does Jesus do? He brings you to his altar and says, "Take and eat. Take and drink. My body, my blood for your forgiveness." And my heart has no escape. At that moment it is just me and Jesus. My bridegroom means *me*!

What Am I Here For?

If your salvation is from first to last *entirely* a gift from God and you can do nothing to earn it with your life, you may be thinking, *"So, what am I here for?"* Again, the Bible gives you the answer: **"Whether you eat or drink or whatever you do, do it all for the glory of God"** (1 Corinthians 10:31). This is the principle that guides every decision you make. Ask yourself, *"How can I give God glory?"*

That desire to give God glory is going to grow and grow the more you are reading and studying God's Word. And if you think about it, where else would we want to be? Imagine you had a world-class chef over to your house and he was preparing your favorite meal. All day long he is making everything from scratch, the aromas are filling the house, and you are salivating. Finally, the chef comes to you and gives you a bite on a fork—it's the best thing you've ever eaten! Would you be content to say, "Well, that's all I need." No! Once you've tasted how good it is, you will of course want more! In fact, you probably wouldn't want anyone watching

> *That desire to give God glory is going to grow and grow the more you are reading and studying God's Word.*

you as you devour the rest!

The same is true once we've tasted how good God's love and forgiveness is in the Bible. First Peter 2:2,3 says, **"Like newborn babies, crave pure spiritual milk** (i.e., the Word of God)**, so that by it you may grow up in your salvation, now that you have tasted that the Lord is good."** Continuing to devour the Word of God will help you give God glory in your life.

So will staying connected to God's people in worship. The writer to the Hebrews says that we should not give up meeting together as some do, but encourage one another—and all the more as you see the day approaching (Hebrews 10:25). As we prepare to meet Jesus, whether at the end of our lives or at the end of the world, it is vital we stay connected to our fellow believers in worship to encourage and be encouraged.

Have you ever grilled with charcoal? What happens to a piece of charcoal that rolls away from the burning pile? It may burn for a while, but eventually it will go out. It no longer has the encouragement of its fellow briquettes. The same is true for Christians. We need the encouragement of others. And never underestimate the encouragement your presence gives, even if you never talk to many who are in church.

I had a member of my congregation who lost

his wife. For four weeks after that he would come to church during the opening hymn and leave before the blessing at the end. I didn't have a chance to encourage him personally, so I stopped by his house. The first thing he told me I had never appreciated before: "Pastor, it's too hard to talk with people at church right now. But I can't tell you how comforting and encouraging it is just to be sitting in church with everyone else." Gathering with your fellow believers in worship will help you give God glory in your life.

You know the reason for the hope that you have. Share it!

As people who know they are going to heaven, we want to share that with everyone else. First Peter 3:15 says, **"In your hearts revere Christ as Lord. Always be prepared to give an answer to everyone who asks you to give the reason for the hope that you have."** Maybe you're thinking, *"But I don't know enough."* Well, that's something to keep growing in through the study of God's Word, but it's no excuse. You know the reason for the hope that you have. Share it!

A great example of that came through my daughter. When she was six years old, I took her to the store. As we were checking out, she blurted out to the clerk, "Did you know that Jesus died on the cross to take away your sins?" I was shocked! I thought, *"Man, I would have first had to get to know the person and break the ice . . ."* My daughter taught me a valuable lesson. I guarantee I knew more than she did about God's Word, but *anyone* can give a reason for the hope that they have—including you! Sharing your faith gives God glory in your life.

Having the proper perspective will also help you give God glory in your life. The apostle Paul says, **"Whoever sows to please the Spirit, from the Spirit will reap eternal life"** (Galatians 6:8). Paul reminds us that through the Spirit, who creates faith in Christ, we **"reap eternal life."** How does the fact that we have eternity before us help us prioritize how we use our time here on this earth?

Picture a time line that goes from 0 to 10,000 years. Plot out your life on that line. It looks like a sliver, doesn't it? Now change that time line to represent 24 hours instead of 10,000 years. Do you know how long that same sliver would represent? About 11 minutes.

Now imagine that you wake up one morning to your alarm and it won't shut off. You hit your head on the headboard as you sit up in bed; your feet hit the cold floor and you jam your toe walking by the baseboard. You go to grab coffee but the coffeemaker is broken; you go to shower but the water heater is out. . . . So, how were your first 11 minutes of that day? Terrible. Now imagine that the whole rest of the day everything goes right— you meet the person of your dreams and fall in love, you win the lottery, you get a promotion at work, and on and on and on. At the end of that day, if I ask you, "So, how was your day?" What would you say? "Oh, I had an awful first 11 minutes"? No! You'd say, "This was the best day of my life!" You wouldn't even be thinking about the first 11 minutes!

The same is true with this life and eternity. Here's what one hymn writer said: "When we've been there ten thousand years . . . we've no less days to sing God's praise than when we'd first begun" (John Newton, "Amazing Grace"). With that perspective, I can give a crazy amount of myself in this life knowing that eternal life awaits me. Having the proper perspective will help you give God glory in your life.

We also need to understand that we don't have to worry. Jesus said, **"See how the flowers of the field grow. They do not labor or spin. Yet I tell you that not even Solomon in all his splendor was dressed like one of these. If that is how God clothes the grass of the field, which is here today and tomorrow is thrown into the fire, will he not much more clothe you—you of little faith?** *So do not worry,* **saying, 'What shall we eat?' or 'What** shall we drink?' or 'What shall we wear?' For the pagans run after all these things, and your heavenly Father knows that you need them. But seek first his kingdom and his righteousness, and all these things will be given to you as well" (Matthew 6:28-33). Jesus uses an argument from the lesser to the greater to show how you don't need to worry.

Value is determined by how much someone is willing to pay for something. How much would you pay for a bag of grass? Nothing! How much did God pay for you? God bought you with the blood of his Son on the cross. If God takes care of grass, which is worth nothing, he most certainly will take care of you, who is worth the priceless blood of Jesus. On top of that, remember that the Father knows what we need even more than we do.

When my two-year-old came to me with a bag of brown sugar and said, "I eat." What did I do? Did I open the bag for her because a loving Father always gives what his children want? No! That would be a terrible father. I gave her a healthy snack because that's what she needed. You don't have a terrible heavenly Father either. He knows what you need. Don't worry. Understanding that helps to give God glory in your life.

That truth helps us with the decisions in our lives. Have you ever had a situation where you didn't know what to do? Of course! The decision between right and something God says is wrong is an easy decision. God gets glory when you pick the right one. But sometimes, even many times in life, we are faced with a decision between right and right. And we feel stuck, as if God wants us to pick the right one and he's just waiting to see if we do. That can be crippling.

One Christian teacher explained it this way. He said, "Every day is Christmas for God." Here's what he meant by that. Say your child wants to get you a Christmas present and he goes to the store to pick one out, but when he gets there he sees two presents that he thinks you'll like. Finally, after weighing out the options, he picks the one on the right, wraps it up, and gives it to you for Christmas. When you open it, what are you going to say? "It's perfect! I love it!" Now what if he would have picked the one on the left? You would say the same thing, "It's perfect! I love it!" Because your child was doing something out of love for you.

The same is true with God. Every day is Christmas for God. He can't wait to see which option between right and right you'll pick. And the one you pick will be the one he blesses . . . either way. I heard someone who lost a friend describe his friend this way, "He was one who lived his whole life constantly in the presence of God."

What a beautiful description of the freedom and confidence of the Christian life. May the same thing be said about our lives! **"Whether you eat or drink or whatever you do, do it all for the glory of God"** (1 Corinthians 10:31).

What Happens When I Die?

We've seen that heaven is given to us by God as a free gift—we contribute nothing for it! We need not fear the end. We've seen that God really will forgive our sins through his Word and sacraments. We need not fear the end. We've seen that we will want to thank God freely with our lives and give him glory—not to appease God but because he is already pleased with us. We need not fear the end.

Then why is there part of me that's still afraid? Well, I still have my sinful nature with its doubts. Sometimes you'll hear people say, "Death is a natural part of life." No it's not! Not when God created us! We were created to live. Death is a violent separation from that original design. I've never died before—there is a fear of the unknown. In this section, let's look at how God calms our fears about death and the Last Day.

Someone once explained that we are dust plus the breath of God and when we die, God takes his breath back. Ecclesiastes 12:7 says, **"And the dust** (i.e., the body) **returns to the ground it came from, and the spirit** (i.e., the soul) **returns to God who gave it."** So when we die, our bodies and souls separate. The body gets buried and becomes dust. What happens to the soul? The writer to the Hebrews says, **"People are destined to die once,**

and after that to face judgment" (Hebrews 9:27).

The soul of a believer in Jesus goes to heaven while the soul of an unbeliever goes to hell. And this happens immediately. There is no "in between" time. Jesus told the repentant thief on the cross, **"Truly I tell you, today you will be with me in paradise"** (Luke 23:43). Finally, on the Last Day when Jesus comes again, everyone's body and soul will be joined again for the final declaration of the judgment that has already taken place for those who died before that day. Jesus said about the Last Day, or judgment day: **"Do not be amazed at this, for a time is coming when all who are in their graves will hear his voice and come out—those who have done what is good will rise to live, and those who have done what is evil will rise to be condemned"** (John 5:28,29).

> Faith is never alone. There will always be evidence of that faith in what we do.

But I thought the Bible says that we will be judged on the basis of faith and not on the basis of our deeds? That is correct. Ephesians 2:8 says, **"It is by grace you have been saved, through faith—and this is not from yourselves, it is the gift of God."** We are saved by the faith that God gives us. However, can you see faith? In one sense, no. Faith is a matter of the heart known only to God. However, in another sense, yes. Faith can be seen by what I do. We are saved by faith alone, not works. But faith is never alone. There will always be evidence of that faith in what we do.

Listen to what Jesus will say on the Last Day to believers—some of the most beautiful words in all of Scripture: **"Come, you who are blessed by my Father; take your inheritance, the kingdom prepared for you since the creation of the world. For I was hungry and you gave me something to eat, I was thirsty and you gave me something to drink, I was a stranger and you invited me in, I needed clothes and you clothed me, I was sick and you looked after me, I was in prison and you came to visit me"** (Matthew 25:34-36).

Notice that since faith can't be seen in the heart, Jesus will point to how faith did show itself in actions. How do you know? Well, answer this. What is missing in Jesus' listing? There is no mention of sin! Why not? Because for the believer, all the imperfections in those actions have been washed away! All that remains is a good work done out of love for Jesus.

Here's the truth of every good work we do: There is at least some sin in every one of them. We never have a perfectly pure motive. When my daughter wakes up at 5:00 A.M. and comes to my side of the bed and says, "I breakfast." Is my first thought, *"Oh wonderful, my child, whom I love, is awake and wants breakfast. I will get right up and make her something!"* Are you kidding? No way! I'm thinking, *"Seriously? You're awake already? I just want to sleep!"* And I'll ignore her until her persistence makes me abandon all hope of going back to sleep. I'll get up and grudgingly make her some breakfast.

That is a heavily sin-tainted good work! But here's the beautiful thing: on the Last Day, Jesus will display that work as evidence of faith because he goes on to say, **"Whatever you did for one of the least of these . . . you did for me"** (Matthew 26:40). The sin of that good work was washed away, and all that remains is the good.

Also, don't miss the kinds of things Jesus *will* list. He doesn't say, "For you gave millions of dollars to the poor and you started a charity and you volunteered 40 hours a week at church." No, he points to giving food, giving drink, helping the sick, etc. He points to what we so often think is mundane and unimportant. There is no mundane in the service of a Christian.

Our Christian lives do not go unnoticed by our Savior. When I change my child's diaper, you will likely not read about it in tomorrow's *New York Times*, but that doesn't make it unimportant. All that matters is that it is written in the *Heavenly Times* and Jesus is showing the angels the headline, "Dad changes diaper!" They all think it's marvelous because it was done out of love for Jesus.

On the other hand, listen to the words Jesus will speak to unbelievers on the Last Day—some of the most awful words in all of Scripture: **"Depart from me, you who are cursed, into the eternal fire . . . for I was hungry and you gave me nothing to eat, I was thirsty and you gave me nothing to drink"** (Matthew 25:41,42). Wait a minute! I know lots of unbelievers who feed their kids, give them drinks of water, and so on. How can Jesus say this? It's because of what we just covered. There is some sin, some selfish motive, in every good work we do. For the unbeliever who rejects Jesus' forgiveness, that sin stain remains, making it evil. And Jesus will tell them to keep walking.

When Is the Last Day Going to Happen?

There are many people who have predicted the day . . . and there are many people who were wrong. I remember billboards up on the freeway near my house that warned of the Last Day coming on December 21, 2012. Well, at the time of this writing, we are well into 2016! Second Peter 3:10 says, **"But the day of the Lord will come like a thief."** When do expect to be robbed by a thief? Monday, Tuesday? No, a person never knows. So what do we do? We are prepared all the time. We lock our doors, we lock our cars, we keep our money in banks, and so on.

What does that tell you about preachers who claim to know when the Last Day is? They're false. Jesus told us that no one knows the day or hour. As a student, if you knew you had a test on Friday, when would you start studying? You'd probably start Thursday . . . maybe even Friday on the bus! How prepared are you for that test? Not very. Jesus wants us always to be prepared. He doesn't want us to think, *"Well, the Last Day is still 40 years off, so I'll get serious about Christianity then."* No, he wants us always to be prepared for when he will glorify our weak bodies and take us to heaven with him.

Philippians 3:21 says, **"Who, by the power that enables him to bring everything under his control, will transform our lowly bodies so that they will be like his glorious body."** So what does a glorious body look like? First Corinthians chapter 15 uses words like *imperishable, glorious, powerful, spiritual* . . . okay, so what does that look like? I don't know; I've never seen a glorified body. How old will you be? What age would you pick? When I've asked that question to others, most say 25, but I know of one who said his ideal age was 55! The answer is that we won't have age, because we will be living in eternity.

I don't know what age we will appear. But this I know, it's going to be great! It's like getting a Christmas present from your spouse—are you nervous that you won't like it when you open it? No! You're going to love it because it comes from someone who loves you and wants to please you!

When most people hear terms like *Last Day* and *judgment day*, what emotion is strongest? For most people, there is an idea of fear behind "meeting their Maker." But listen to how God wants us to use this beautiful truth of the Last Day: **"We do not want you to be uninformed about those who sleep in death, so that you do not grieve like the rest of mankind, who have no hope"** (1 Thessalonians 4:13).

Let's pause there. Do you know the way the

Bible describes death for a believer? It says believers "fall asleep." Remember that the "wages of sin is death." But for a believer, all sin has been taken away, so a believer doesn't die in that sense; they merely fall asleep in this life and wake up in heaven.

The account goes on to describe the Last Day: Jesus will come with a loud command, with the voice of an archangel, and the believers will rise from the dead. Those who are still alive will be with the Lord forever. Then it finishes like this: **"Therefore, encourage one another with these words"** (1 Thessalonians 4:18). God wants the truth of the Last Day to fill us with hopeful anticipation, not fearful dread!

How does the truth of the Last Day make an impact on our lives today? When I was younger and knew that I was going to Great America theme park at the end of the week, do you think that truth impacted my life that week? You bet!

First, I was excited all week because I had something incredible to look forward to. Second, I told people about it because I was so excited about it. Third, you better believe I wanted to behave knowing that my parents were giving me a gift like that!

You're going somewhere way better than Great America! You're going to live in perfect bliss in heaven all because of Jesus. So do you need to fear the end? That's an easy answer for a Christian: Because of Jesus, absolutely not!

About the Writer

David Scharf served as a pastor in Greenville, Wisconsin, and now serves as a professor of theology at Martin Luther College in Minnesota. He has presented at numerous leadership, outreach, and missionary conferences across the country. Dave and his wife have six children ages 4-14.

About Time of Grace

Time of Grace is for people who want more growth and less struggle in their spiritual walk. Through the timeless truth of God's Word, we connect people to God's grace so they know they are loved and forgiven and so they can start living in the freedom they've always wanted.

To discover more, please visit timeofgrace.org or call 800.661.3311.

Help share God's message of grace!

Every gift you give helps Time of Grace reach people around the world with the good news of Jesus. Your generosity and prayer support take the gospel of grace to others through our ministry outreach and help them find the restart with Jesus they need.

Give today at timeofgrace.org/give or by calling 800.661.3311.

Thank you!